Glimpses

Gary Beck

ISBN: 978-93-6354-886-2

First Edition: 2025
Rs. 200/-

Cyberwit.net
HIG 45 Kaushambi Kunj, Kalindipuram
Allahabad - 211011 (U.P.) India
http://www.cyberwit.net
Tel: +(91) 9415091004
E-mail: info@cyberwit.net

Printed at Repro India Limited.

To Debbie, a bright light that reflects her talent, skill and abilities
all in good spirit

Books by Gary Beck

Novels

Acts of Defiance
Extreme Change
Flawed Connections
Call to Valor
Sudden Conflicts
Crumbling Ramparts
Flare Up
Raise High the Walls
Still Defiant
State of Rage
Wave Length
Protective Agency
Obsess
Still Obsessed
Rescue Me
Until the Bell
Rescue Others

Poetry Collections

Expectations
Days of Destruction
Dawn in Cities
Assault on Nature
Songs of a Clerk
Civilized Ways
Conditioned Response
Displays
Perceptions
Fault Lines
Tremors
Unillumined
Perturbations
Blossoms of Decay
Rude Awakenings
Blunt Force
Remission of Order
Contusions
Transitions
Earth Links
Mortal Coil
Desperate Seeker
Too Harsh For Pastels
Temporal Dreams
Severance
Redemption Value
Fractional Disorder
Disruptions
Ignition Point
Learning Curve
Resonance
Turbulence
Lacerations
State of the Union
Purpose
Double Envelopment
Unveilings
Discoveries
Virtual Living
Molecular Distortion
Glimpses

Play Collections

The Big Match and other one act plays
Collected Plays of Gary Beck Volume I
Collected Plays of Gary Beck Volume II
Collected Plays of Gary Beck Volume III

Translations

Four Plays by Jean Baptiste Moliere (Directed by Gary Beck)
Three Plays by Aristophanes (Directed by Gary Beck)
Sophocles-Three Plays (Directed by Gary Beck)
Agamemnon: The Play by Aeschylus (Directed by Gary Beck)

Short Story Collections

A Glimpse of Youth and other stories
Now I Accuse and other stories
Dogs Don't Send Flowers and other stories
Judgments and other stories

Essays

The Republic of Dreams and other essays
Collected Essays

Poems from 'Glimpses' have appeared in:

Bindweed Magazine, Dissident Voice, Highland Park Poetry, Madswirl, Modern Literature, Open Door Magazine, Poetry Catalog, Polseguera Magazine, Setu Bilingual Magazine, Syndic Literary Journal, Taj Mahal Review, The Deronda Review, The Nashwaak Review, The Poetry Magazine, The Seventh Quarry Poetry Magazine, VerbalArts Magazine (Author Press), Winamop Magazine, Zin Daily.

Contents

Madness Reigns

We send our children to school
never expecting
a troubled youth
will go on a rampage,
open fire,
murder
precious offspring.

We go to a rock concert
never expecting
a troubled man
will find a vantage point,
open fire,
murder
innocent concertgoers.

Throughout our troubled land
we gather in public places
never expecting
a demented individual
will open fire,
murder people
who dared to get together.

Desperation

I saw a news item
about Afghanistan
on tv
showing a poor family
that sold its children
to get something to eat.

I found myself thinking
what I would do
if my family was starving,
but quickly realized
there was a world of difference
between my country,
however declined and divided,
the land of opportunity,
at least for some,
where I could get a service job,
become a delivery boy,
find some way to make a few bucks'

Steal? It would have to be for food.
I wouldn't know how to sell anything else.
Sell drugs? Where would I get it?
Sell my body? That made me laugh.
This desiccated old thing?
But that's crazy thinking.
There's always a food bank.

Afghanistan is different
than the good old U.S.A.
There really are families
without resources, starving,
who decided, however callous
it might seem to others,
to sell their children
so they could eat.

No matter how hard I tried
I couldn't picture their way of life
well enough to conclude
if what they did was right or wrong.
I can only believe
no matter what happened
I'd never sell my children.

Last Threads

I lie in illness bed
and do not know
if I will live
to see the next dawn.
Too tired to think,
images past
creep through my head…
A waterfall
I stood under
with lively friends,
a bird concerto
the first night in the woods,
singing until the darkness faded.
So much beauty
I was fortunate to see
that I cannot regret
imminent departure.

Voting Rites

Election day, U.S.A.,
and almost no protests,
rioting, violence,
making some of us remember
we're not Russia or China
and we still have
some democracy
and we can cast our ballots
for the candidate of choice,
if there is a choice
to maintain the fabric
of a free society.

Encroachment

When most wars start
aggressors don't expect
a disastrous end.
Persia, Athens, Rome,
Germany, Japan,
sent destruction
beyond their borders,
then suffered total defeat,
mass casualties less important
than loss of power
for eager war mongers
whose dreams of conquest
were harshly shattered.

Endemic Decay

I sit hunched
in my personal wheelchair
in the impersonal waiting room
of the geriatric clinic,
spine surrendering to old age,
no longer holding up
my unresponsive head.
I barely notice the nurse
taking me to the exam room,
where a few minutes later
the doctor cheerfully enters,
does not examine me,
tells me with a smile:
"Nothing has changed since last time.
There are no new treatments.
Come back in four months.
Maybe there'll be something new.
Make an appointment at the desk."
I barely notice the nurse
take me to the waiting room.
My personal care attendant
makes the next appointment,
wheels me outside to the street,
puts me in the van, drives home,
helps me into bed,
puts out the lights, closes the door,
forgets me for a while.

I lie there barely cognizant
but manage to ask myself:
"Do I want to live like this
for another four months?"

Radiology

No one waiting is relaxed.
The particle bombardment
an intrusive procedure,
not as messy as cutting,
but serious
or they wouldn't be here.
All are still masked,
pandemic regulations
enforced in the hospital.
Some sit rigidly,
others twitching, feet pumping,
eyes staring in apprehension
when a doctor walks by.
The clerks are indifferent
to people's fears
and tension grows
without offers of comfort,
the only recourse
patient resignation.

Historical Reminder

In 341 B.C.
Pericles of Athens
made a funeral oration
to commemorate the dead
in the first year of the war
between Sparta and Athens.
He spoke about the value
of democracy, asserting
'happiness depends on being free'.

Athens was divided
between peace and war,
differing factions,
one for democracy
the other for tyrants.
Their system was imperfect
as are all human endeavors,
yet they didn't violently oppose
contrary beliefs,
but settled them in assembly.

I think about their achievement,
rule of the people
in a time of kings,
a gift to mankind
that took millennia
to appear again
and compare it to my land,
implacably divided

in a complex society
with so many issues
that the only way to survive
will be to learn to get along.

Perhaps our schools
could teach our youngsters
a few lessons from the past
including Pericles who said,
'We are free and tolerant
in our private lives,
but in public affairs
we obey the law'.
Few of our elders

work for the public good
and they will not change,
so it's up to youth
to preserve our future,
before it's too late.

Entertainment

Western civilization
is more connected
media wise, socially,
than third world countries,
so important events
war, famine, plague,
have more impact
almost instantly,
a major innovation
over smoke signals,
the heliograph,
the telegraph,
for full frontal disasters,
live and in color,
24/7,
for our viewing pleasure.

Worries

I go to the hospital
to get a booster shot
to protect me from Covid.
I'm the only patient.
The waiting room feels strange,
as if we abandoned
the doctors and nurses
who helped us through the plague.
People stopped wearing masks,
they're not distancing,
so fears of close contact
seem crazy to them,
no longer concerned
with possible illness.
They won't take precautions,
I can't force them to,
so I'll still be peculiar
when they think they're normal.

Audio Threat

The sounds of war
terrify
helpless citizens
in unsafe shelters
who hear the shrieks
of missiles, bombs, cannon shells,
freezing their minds,
pounding their bodies
when loud explosions
detonate nearby,
none differentiating
between civilians
and combatants,
all at risk
of sudden death.

Self Destruction

I sit by the East River
on a sunny Spring morning,
the water no longer clean.
The current brings human waste
to the polluted ocean
that will take longer to taint
than smaller waterways,
succumbing more quickly
to the inundation
of so much detritus
that we may not save
the liquid of life.

Emergency Room

I watch the ill, the frightened,
the diseased, the demented,
huddling in the waiting room,
devastated beyond hope.
Only sad resignation
keeps them from collapse,
dissolving into disfunction.
Only vestiges remain
to define a human being,
at least remnants of one.

Betrayed Citizens

The owners of America
spend much to misinform us
in order to divide us.
Media manipulations
successfully deceive us
and we seethe with anger
at those different from us,
allowing hatred to blind us
until we cannot see
our true enemy,
corporations swollen
with excessive profits,
rewarding their lackeys,
rejecting the rest of us
from human consideration,
while the arrogant 1%
build bigger chateaus,
refuse to pay their fair share
to help a struggling nation.

Distractions

Primitive man
kept eyes, ears, nose,
wide open,
always on the alert
for life and death threats
always abounding
in a hostile environment.
And the hunter/gatherers
didn't wear headsets,
text, look at screens,
for at any moment
danger might strike.

Requests

Everyone wants money,
so many causes
it's hard to imagine
how they hope to raise funds
from the diminishing,
overly demanded on
middle class.
Most of them ask for
19 dollars a month,
Elephants, Polar Bears,
disadvantaged children,
wounded warriors…
The list goes on and on,
all are worthy,
some more than others.
I can never decide
which to respond to.
All are needy,
but there are so many
I tune them out
and wait impatiently
for my show to continue.

Ceremony

Another President
lays a wreath
on the Tomb of the Unknown Soldier.
I have seen this many times
over the years
by many Presidents,
but the bugle playing Taps
is still the loneliest sound
in the world.

Ode to Mass Shootings

America, the violent
with more mass murders
than authoritative states,
with more attacks on the innocent
a media bonanza
that celebrates the suffering
of those who lost loved ones.
The worst occurrences
are at schools,
where despite preparations
they are rarely ready
for sudden invasion,
a gunman opening fire,
instant panic,
a few remain calm
protecting others,
while any hope of normalcy
evaporates
in an insane land.

Tomorrow

Many of us live in high rises,
at least those still privileged.
The mass of our citizens
live in decrepit housing
still somewhat better
than the plight of the homeless,
existing marginally
wherever they can,
children automatically doomed
by non-comforting environment,
some with initial success
through their smart phones
if they're lucky enough to get one.
They may not play learning games,
but they know how to push buttons
that may give some a chance
for work in the service industry,
the biggest employer
now that the government
has diminished functions
for a sure percentage
of the taxpayer class,
only the 1% of consequence,
the miniscule middle class
struggles to retain comforts,
the working poor easily discarded,
everyone else callously dismissed
having lost intrinsic value
to an inbred oligarchy.

American River

Depending on the time of day
the river is drab brown, black,
another polluted waterway
courtesy of a people
who don't seem to care
the once clear blue river
is now so murky
you cannot see
below the tainted surface
that flows and flows
just as it always did,
but now carrying toxins
to *the* no longer blue sea.

Sore Loser

We've gradually lost
gracious losers
and it's become usual
when the decision
doesn't go your way
to object, protest, lie,
curse the system
that you celebrate
when it goes your way,
finally reaching the stage
where you'll destroy democracy
because you didn't win.

Rich Journey

My declining senses
remind me,
before it's too late
to remember the beauty,
natural, man made,
I have been fortunate enough
to savor,
bird songs on a Spring day,
exquisite Beethoven,
surely the highest level
of human creation.
So many pleasures
there is not time
to recollect so many.
When I depart,
I know not when
no complaints
for wondrous gifts
beyond imagining.

Perceptions

Many Americans believe
the Capitol Building,
our seat of government,
should not be invaded
by an aggressive mob
whose intention
is to prevent
the electoral process
confirming a president.
When the invasion includes
violent break ins,
ferocious assaults
on the defending police,
dangerous threats
to our legislators,
this is insurrection.
Repeated videos
of brutal attacks
now called:
'Legitimate Political Discourse',
ignored or denied
by a legion of the blind
pushing the extreme
of the 'Big Lie',
in order to convince
the disaffected
Democracy is obsolete
and should be replaced

by an autocrat,
however unworthy,
however unqualified
to lead a great nation
in a time of peril.

Blind to Reason

Democracy at best
is a fragile creation,
always at risk
from greedy intruders
urgent to fondle power,
deluding themselves
they're meant to rule,
enticing others
dissatisfied
the way things are,
too short sighted
to let time heal
wounds real or imagined
with freedom's medication,
abandoning the Constitution
for calls to violence,
preferring to destroy
that which we have,
too ignorant to know
overthrow of the state
by the exploiters
only leads to chaos,
the painful end
of the American dream.

Perplexed

Many of us
do not understand
why vaccinations,
a preventive of disease
has been a rights issue.
Many of us
do not know
where in scripture
the Lord says:
Thou shalt not
be vaccinated.
So let the virus
run rampant,
kill millions,
disrupt economies,
devastate nations,
as long as the few
can resist the many
regardless of consequences.

Rumors of War

The Russians (not Soviets)
mass on the Ukrainian border
threatening invasion
with guns, tanks, planes,
advanced weaponry,
while the U.S. growls
thinking sanctions
a guaranteed tool
that will only punish,
the poor, the middle class,
while oligarchs
from both countries
bloated with indulgences
wage fierce battles
at Sothby auctions.

Tomorrow II

Those who can afford it
live in skyscrapers,
most high enough
not to see squalor below.
When they travel
they take aircars
from elevated platforms
so they do not interact
with the underclass.
And if they manage carefully
they will not have to notice
the suffering of the people
removed from privilege.

Hang Together

We no longer hold some truths
to be self evident.
Not that everyone believed them,
but there were decent men and women
idealistic enough to accept
all men are created equal.
We do come out the same way
from similar places,
but the vitriol of difference
overshadows tolerance
and many have chosen
the path of anger and hate,
rather than recognize
that when blue lizards
with ray guns, from Tau Ceti,
come to exterminate
what they consider
alien humanity,
it might be too late
to get along
for the common good.

Response Patterns

Plague changes our attitudes,
Most for the better,
some stay the same
a few get worse.
Pressures on the poor
often lead to increased crime,
envy for what others have
frequently promoting
all sorts of robberies,
some of them violent.

Street behavior changes.
Some are more polite
shared danger bringing closeness.
Others are more aggressive
refusing to move aside
so others can get by
without being shouldered.
The courtesy of some
a refreshing reminder
of the inherent goodness
of most of humanity.

Ask Not

The rate of expansion
of the service sector
where most Americans work
is at a record high
despite supply chain problems.
It's consoling to know
that more and more of us
toil at low-paying jobs
that we're still glad to get
as long as we need to eat,
keeping us too tired
after demanding days
to protest inequity
between haves and have nots.

Ode to Central Park

Green relief station
for concrete exiles
far from nature,
letting us see birds,
walk on grass,
breathe cleaner air
than exhaust pipe streets,
runners, bikers, dog walkers,
a large springtime flock
of Canadian geese
graze like cattle
on fenced in lawns,
tourists feeding turtles
in a teeming pond,
small jazz groups
with blaring horns, pounding drums,
a lonely cellist
bowing for acoustics
by the underpass,
something for almost everyone,
a city refuge.

Coincidence?

We survived the Cold War,
though a few times
obliteration murmured
and defeated the Soviet Union
by outspending the big, bad, bear.
Yet ongoing threats
to American security
changed the nation,
gave the oligarchs
opportunity
to consolidate wealth,
move industry offshore
so we no longer made things,
moved the people off the land
into unwelcoming cities,
subsistence taken for granted,
as long as trucks keep delivering
food, other necessities,
power keeps flowing
to sustain cliff dwellers
dependent on electronics.
The bond of community
is perilously frayed,
except for dwindling
good citizens
who want to help neighbors.
We eat in isolation rooms
diverted by tv, the internet,
less active than our fathers,

less willing to face the fascists
overturning our society,
vandals eroding the constitution,
thugs violating the law,
crumbling infrastructure
eroding travel, country
and our non staturous leaders
can not turn the tide
of incipient disaster.

Disease

Traditionally,
doctors knew best
and for a while
we obeyed their instructions,
except for the stubborn,
the dimmer resisters.
Then insurance companies
inserted themselves
into health treatment,
determining how much they paid
medical practitioners,
severing direct relations
to payer and payee,
restricting how much
insurance paid,
thus changing a profession
once independent
now servants of actuarial tables.

Criminals

I'm not as bad
as Vladimir Putin,
Kim Jong Un,
many others.
What I've done wrong
cannot compare
to men of great evil,
yet my wrongdoing
weighs heavier on me
than the great crimes
inflicted on the innocent
by human-rights abusers.

Excursion

I was walking on a mountain side
brooding about my failures,
dissatisfaction
the primary motivation
for a new direction,
answers elusive,
spurring frustration,
oblivious
to a beautiful Spring day,
when I came upon
a wild blackberry bush
bursting with large berries.
I picked and picked,
ate and ate
until sated,
went back to my cabin
nothing resolved,
but filled with great feelings
for Nature's bounty.

Confusion

One day it's warm
and the sparrows sing:
"It's Spring. It's Spring."
The next day it's cold
and the sparrows cry:
"What happened to Spring?"
In early January
the trees were budding
though winter was young.
So many of us
bred on concrete streets
do not notice
seasonal disorders,
or we'd surely know
the climate is a changing.

Motives

War is rarely righteous
most caused by greed,
the lust for power,
economic expansion,
many other reasons,
few are noble.
Only innocent countries
that defend themselves
against foreign invasion
may have honest cause.
Rebels invariably
want to replace
the current system
to gain the benefits
of wealth and privilege.
Patriotic wars
to defend the homeland
from foreign aggression
must be admired
for the resultant sacrifices
from the call to duty.

Tomorrow III

The nation lives in fear
painfully revealed daily
as the great separation,
malevolent conspiracy
contrived by the 1%,
or corporate acquisitions
devouring resources
meant to serve the people,
now semi-paralyzed
by implacable divisions
fostered by the media,
following the guidance
of unscrupulous leaders
who gain in influence
the further we're apart.
The hope of democracy
that many still believe in
seems to erode faster
as the trumpets of hate
resonate in the land.

Disorder in the Land

Shootings wreck the nation,
hundreds killed,
hundreds wounded,
one lunatic after another
with a semi-automatic weapon
murdering Americans
in church, school, supermarket,
while those with power
to prevent the demented
from getting guns
refuse to act.
Some claim citizen's rights,
others in the pay
of the righteous NRA,
with most of us afraid to see
an evil conspiracy
to keep our country distressed
so the lords of profit
continue undisturbed
as they accumulate
more and more wealth
that allows them control
of the people's fate

Assault on Sovereignty

Flights of missiles
devastate the Ukraine
as modern warfare
sweeps the cities
killing civilians,
leveling buildings.
Determined citizens
huddle in the ruins,
listen to their father's tales
of Nazi atrocities
in World War II
almost forgotten,
until the brutal Russians
launched multiple attacks
that did not prevent
furious resistance
by a united people.

Contrasts

Legislators demand
action against Russia
to punish them
for the invasion of Ukraine,
invoking genocide,
war crimes, brutality,
violation of human rights,
with U.S. intervention.
Retired Generals
mostly forgotten
until media trots them out
to talk about war somewhere.
Fortunately, most of them
are practical realists
and remind viewers
Russia is armed
with thousands of nukes
and we can't go charging in
no matter how just the cause,
to risk nuclear conflict.

America the Bountiful

I can never understand
my peculiar country
where millions are hungry
in a prosperous land,
our dedicated congresspersons
would rather fight each other
than help our needy people,
as millions resist vaccination,
confusing rights and religion
with health considerations.
So many complex issues
defining our nation
that opts for conflict
instead of solution
to urgent problems,
while American casinos
won more money in 2021
than ever before,
setting a record
for unproductivity.

Non-Stop Assault

Winter is wearing us down
and it's only been a month
of freezing days, colder nights,
a further affliction
getting Covid
that has depleted so many
as new variants spring up
adding to the stress
that already chafes people
wearing masks, distancing
working and eating at home
fearing the possible spread
of a deadly virus
sweeping the land
of overwhelmed hospitals
desperately waiting for
an end to the pandemic.

Protection

As long as we are shielded
by the rule of law
from the oppressions
we do to each other,
however we name the system
it should benefit all.

Warnings

American Presidents
have frequently faced
all kinds of crises
testing their will
to serve the people.
The most complicated,
the Civil War,
that threatened to end
the United States,
only resolved
by bloody battle,
death and destruction.
We are now in a time
when conflicting beliefs
fueled by an autocrat,
endanger the future
of our divided land
and the growing peril
of violent dissension
troubles those of us
who still have hope
for the American dream.

Land of Liberty

It didn't matter
in the 1940's,
just after World War II,
that the oligarchs
owned the country
since they tolerated
good earnings
for the blue collar class,
though always wary
of demands for more.

Higher education
was the stepping stone
for the men who came home
from bloody war
who wanted a better life.
College degrees
were the passport
to the middle class
and for a short while
all was well.

The newly prosperous
bought homes, cars, appliances,
moved out of cities
into suburbs,
commuted to work
on reliable transportation,
got married, had children,

were comfortable,
but human nature persisted
and greed possessed many.

Although there was enough for all
the oligarchs didn't like
too much acquisition
from the pushy middle class
who always wanted more,
even buying fine art,
which cannot be allowed
by the owners of our land,
who refuse to accept
economic equality.

Arrivals

In science fiction films
alien attackers
are almost always
reptilian based,
or insectoid,
despite superior tech
invariably defeated
by resourceful humans.
When aliens come
in humanoid form
it's to warn or threaten
about ravaging the Earth.
Hollywood neglects
a different visitor,
an explorer or trader ship,
preferring vast fleets
that somehow found
our small planet
in an obscure solar system,
in a remote galaxy.

Tomorrow IV

I go to the refrigerator
that's almost empty.
No milk, butter, eggs,
just a piece of stale cheese.
The supply lines aren't working.
I sit in my cubicle,
designated space, 87 square feet,
which I'm lucky to have,
considering how many
are living on the street.
If I have the internet
I can continue working,
earn enough to pay my rent,
earn enough to keep eating
as long as the delivery drivers
bring food to distribution centers.
So I'll subsist for a while longer
with little hope for the future.

Tolerance Question

If we would be
a democracy
we must get along
with everybody.

Steppingstones

Two-thirds of American workers
without college degrees
lost the opportunity
to become middle class,
as seven and a half million jobs
will no longer take applicants
solely based on merit.
Thus the able
may be ultimately rejected
for an inept paper pusher
who got a degree,
but can't do the job.

Contrasts II

The war in the Ukraine
        rages on,
artillery, missiles
bombarding the cities.
In the good old U.S.A.
We celebrate St. Patrick's Day,
        no one bombs us,
as our legislators demand
we stop the big, bad Russians,
while our retired Generals
warn us about threats of World War III
                if we intervene
and establish a no fly zone
to protect the Ukraine
that will surely lead
to air to air combat
between usn's and themun's,
with the terrifying chance
of nuclear escalation.

Supportive

New York State
is about to issue
the first 100 licenses
to sell legal marijuana
to former arrestees
for selling marijuana.
Progressive legislators
supplementing their initiatives
arranged for SUNY
to offer degree programs
in marijuana studies
with automatic credit
for life experience.
New matriculates
can get B.A.s
in management
for operating street sellers,
art and design
for packaging pot.
The list goes on
proving vindication
for those who said:
'Stay in school'.

Failed States

Empires,
more than other systems
conquer other countries,
indifferent to sovereignty,
first using military force
then economic power,
establishing
a cooperative government
that never has
the loyalty of the people.
Anger grows
at foreign occupiers,
resistance spreads,
efforts to suppress
armed uprisings
become more brutal
as the people unite
against a foreign foe.
Sooner or later
the will to remain
in violent control
of a defeated nation
begins to crumble
and the invader withdraws,
leaving behind
a broken structure
unable to govern
victorious freedom fighters
who cannot build

a functioning state,
chaos and corruption
predominate
as the losers sail away,
no longer concerned
with the failed state.

Medical Practice

Centuries ago
doctors didn't know
how to treat plagues
and the usual cures,
bloodletting, leeches
didn't avail
at a time of travail.
We don't know
if the family physician
said: 'Rest, stay warm,
drink plenty of fluids',
in lieu of prescriptions
that just caused complications.
They wore weird masks
more to repel devils
than prevent disease
in the desperate effort
to ward off
the visit of death.

Aftermath

The plague is almost over.
At least that's what people think.
We stopped getting booster shots
of the vaccine that saved us
from serious illness.
We stopped wearing masks, distancing,
although Covid keeps coming back.
We'll be unprepared
at the next viral outbreak,
so we can only hope
it won't devastate the land.

Tomorrow V

Illness and disease,
accident and injury
have become so widespread
hospitals can no longer afford
to treat non-paying patients,
so millions of Americans
deprived of health services
do not know
who to blame
for the sufferings
that inflict so many.

Dangerous Eruption

Another war rages
on a troubled planet,
this time in Europe
which has known peace
for many years,
battle erupting
and distressing the West
that blithely accepts combat
in Africa, the Mid East,
with only pro forma outrage
as long as it's far away.
When a neighbor is invaded
this disrupts the status quo
of nearby nations
with fragile sovereignty
afraid if one is conquered
they may be next.

The Hospital

Another virus
ravages the land.
the staff are overwhelmed,
demanded on
month after month,
providing care
no matter how tired,
yet everyone I meet
is cheerful, efficient,
a reassuring experience
in a time of pandemic.

Mad or Sane?

Rioters attempt
to violently prevent
the legal transition
of democratic government.
The quality of air, water,
constantly deteriorates,
but it would cut business profits
if they tried to improve it.
The economy booms
for a limited group,
while the rest of us
creep towards poverty.
Crime, drugs, violence,
besiege our cities
apparently allowed
to control the people.
No matter how bad it gets
we have endless distractions
on the internet, tv,
of mind numbing sports shows.
Mad or Sane?

St. Val…

Romance
has never been
part of my character,
separating me
from beauties wanting
flowers, perfume,
other tokens celebrating
a certain day,
whose sentiment is alien
to my sensibility.

Braying

Some elected officials
angrily call for help
for the beleaguered Ukraine.
Of course they won't risk their lives,
but they demand no-fly zones,
though it will confront Russia
in air to air combat
that if Russia loses
could lead to escalation,
possible nuclear exchange
and our legislators
are too stupid to realize
they may be provoking
World War III.

Playing With Fire

Russia launched
an unjust war
targeting the Ukraine,
which bravely resists
the deadly assault,
citizens defending their soil
armed and united,
while the desperate leader
calls the world for help
to save his country
from a ruthless aggressor.
Any decent person
is outraged at the attack
on a peaceable country,
but sending military aid,
no matter our sympathies,
can challenge Russian resolve
that can never be allowed
to escalate
to nuclear war.

Naked Aggression

The unprovoked attack
on helpless Ukraine
kills innocent civilians
as invading Russians
devastate the land.
Motivation is questionable,
revive the lost empire,
capture the food source,
exercise power,
intimidate neighbors.
Whatever the reason
the threat is constant
for unexpected escalation
that might erupt
into nuclear exchange.

Invasion

In ancient times
there may not have been advance notice
that an army was coming
to conquer your country.
The formation of nation states
brought improved communications
and sometimes your enemy
declared war before attacking.
The Information Age
with sophisticated media,
satellite transmissions
of troop movements
makes it difficult
to sneak troops across frontiers
so they know you're coming,
they just can't defeat you.
The victims must rely
on the age old assistance
of imperial overreach
and failure to suppress
determined resistance
not to give in
to alien invaders.

High Peril

Nuclear weapons
were very primitive
in the 1940's,
difficult to deliver
and there weren't many.
But stockpiles grew and grew,
delivery systems improved
until there were only minutes
before a strike arrived.
The non-state actors
who hated the West
clamoring for nukes
to destroy the infidel crusaders,
a wonder of our times...
They haven't bought any... Yet.
The biggest miracle
no nuclear exchange
during the Cold War.
So many forget
the never ending danger
when so many countries
have huge arsenals
aimed at each other,
ignored by most,
going about their lives,
while weapons of mass destruction
remain in the hands
of unreliable controllers.

Realization

When I was young
I fantasized
about having wisdom,
then benevolently solving
the problems of the world.
Now that I am old
I'm just beginning to know
that most of what I learned
has no redeeming value,
so I must strive each day
while there is still time
for better understanding.

Transformation

Russian aggression
has transformed the Ukraine
to a Western nation
as a result of
a brutal invasion.
Sudden concern
for former Slavs
has some fools
urging intervention
on behalf of a victim state,
not understanding
the dangerous threat
of weapons of mass destruction
should deter rash action
and let us use reason,
not violence
to peacefully resolve
an international crime.

Another Spring

Forsythia and Crocus
are blossoming in the park.
Trees are budding
although it's still cold.
Robins are hopping around
preparing for what Robins do.
Despite our depredations
nature has survived
another Winter.

California Here I Come

A local college
in the spirit of doing good
reserved 15 parking places
in the student parking lot
for the homeless students
who can sleep in their cars.

I'm heading for California
where I'll live in a car,
if I can get a car.
Maybe I can eat
in the cafeteria,
talk to other students,
maybe a professor
and it'll be like
getting an education,
not like New York City
where I sleep on cardboard
and scrounge for food.

Dumbing Down

In divided America
issues are so contentious
that agreement is alien
and many would rather fight
than accept other opinions.
We have reached a critical point
where ignorance or evil
prompts celebration,
eradicated
the truth of science.
Fans, followers, the gullible
too often believe what they hear
from a reassuring source
and lack sufficient knowledge
to determine truth from falsehood.
It's a testament to our times
when a football player
talking about health issues
is more convincing to some
then the words of a doctor.

Geo-Politics

The powerful Russian bear
threatens the Ukraine
and the U.S. reacts
invoking sanctions
which only hurt the people,
not the wealthy,
the makers of policy
who are immune
due to a sufficiency
of worldly goods,
so only total war
could disrupt the order of things.
It would certainly be
clinical insanity
to challenge and provoke
the threat of war
that might rapidly expand
to a nuclear exchange
devastating the earth.

Travel Time

Tourists cannot conceive
that a certain wave
of Covid virus
can suddenly spread
while they are holidaying,
killing so many
it's like the middle-ages
when the black plague
swept Europe
devastating the lands,
but the people
had enough sense
to isolate themselves
as much as possible
and didn't need governments
to mandate separation.

Rapacity

An innocent nation
is brutally invaded
by a powerful neighbor,
smashing the illusion
that Europe is stable.
Just like aggressors past
exercising power
through conquest,
Russia launches attacks
throughout the Ukraine,
blazing a path of destruction,
nuclear power plants
dangerously disrupted,
an accident away
from devastation,
a volatile casualty
as sovereignty crumbles.

Madness Unleashed

Another school shooting.
Too many dead children.
Special interests prevent
decisive action to stop
acquisition of guns
by unstable people
determined to rampage
in church, school, grocery store,
until no place is safe
from violent intrusion
that destroys the lives
of the innocent,
unprotected,
unless they can afford
sufficient security
to protect where they go,
while those of poorer means
are undefended
where they shop, worship,
get an education
in a divided land
that allows assault weapons
to be easily purchased
by those intent
on harming others.

Patient's Apprehensions

I sit on the edge
of the hospital bed
waiting for release.
Doctors, nurses, aides
walk by purposefully,
but do not stop.
I begin to get tense
worried they won't let me go
and I'll spend another night
listening to the cries of pain,
the moaning, sobbing anguish
of broken bodies suffering.
I am not as bad off
as those around me
and can only sit silent
as my fears mount
that I may not receive
imminent discharge.

Growing Darkness

I can no longer see
into the heart
of America,
become darkened
with anger, hate, violence
bursting over a land
divided by differences.
This is not the country
I grew up in
where disagreements
still caused bitterness,
but not in everyone
and compromise prevailed
in times of crisis.
Now the owners of our land
turn us against each other,
encouraging conflict
so we will not unite
and take action to correct
the issues that burden us
and restore democracy.

May It Endure

Democracy at best
is a fragile thing,
only held together
by the will of the people,
assaulted daily
by the servants of profit
eager to undermine
the restrictions
that protect the nation
from the greedy.
And when we lapse
from defense of freedom
as all of us do
sooner or later,
we must be ever watchful
of the avaricious
who scheme while we sleep.

Encroachment II

War rages in the Ukraine.
Atrocities, massacres
have been common
as a ruthless aggressor
devastates a neighbor.
Reasons for the attack unclear
despite the constant stream
of misleading propaganda.
NATO righteously proclaims
we must help the Ukraine,
'even though it's Eastern
it's still European',
not a third world country
where we often intervene
with only mild objections
from the European Union
if it doesn't hurt us.
Even the Germans will react
to war almost next door.
And the good old U.S.A.
always ready to accuse
someone else for violations
of human rights, forgetting
the glass house we live in.

www.ingramcontent.com/pod-product-compliance
Lightning Source LLC
LaVergne TN
LVHW091120150826
845673LV00002B/900
9789363548862